12 Steps to Heaven

my first
impressions of
sex

illustrations by Bernice Lum
text by Tuppy Owens

step1: desire

step 2: foreplay: up there

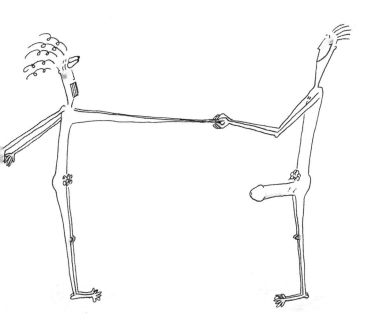

step 3 : foreplay : down there

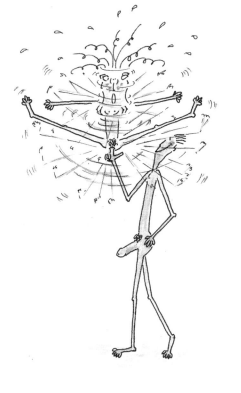

Step 4: lubrication

Step 5 : blowjob

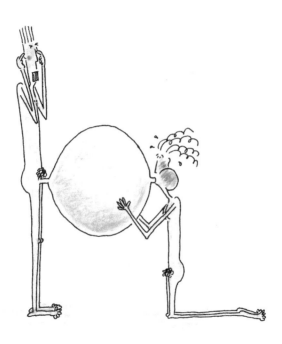

step 6: intercourse

Step 1 : Satisfaction

step 8 : passion

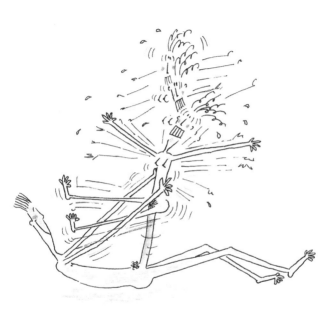

step 9: expertise

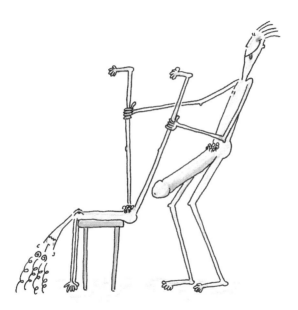

step 10: vaginismus *

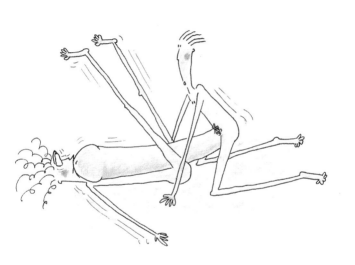

step 11 : deep throat

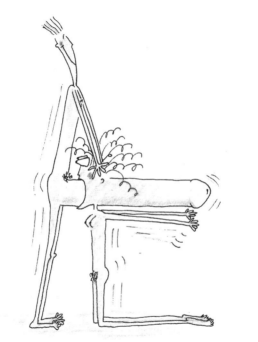

step 12: orgasm

Also available:

MORE STEPS TO HEAVEN
by Bernice Lum
@ £2.95 plus 50p p&p

and

THE SAFER SEX MANIAC'S DIARY
by Tuppy Owens @ £4.95 plus 50p p&p

THE SAFER SEX MANIAC'S BIBLE
by Tuppy Owens @ £4.95 plus 50p p&p

THE SEX MANIAC'S ADDRESS BOOK
by Tuppy Owens @ £4.95 plus 50p p&p

Cheques to Tuppy Owens, PO Box 4ZB, London W1A 4ZB

or from your local bookstore

12 Steps to Heaven
ISBN 1 872819 00 1
Copyright © 1990 Bernice Lum

Published by Tuppy Owens P O Box 4ZB, London W1A 4ZB
Printed in Spain

Illustrations by Bernice Lum
Text by Tuppy Owens